JUST COMMI T SERIES

HISTORY FOR BASIC SCHOOL 1 - (BASED ON NEW NACCA GES CURRICULUM)- BY JANIX K. ASARE

HISTORY FOR BS 1 | Janix K. Asare

Table of Contents

<u>COPYRIGHT</u>

First published in Ghana

April: 2022

By Just Commit Foundation

Obuasi

Ashanti, Ghana

Website: justcommit.org   **Email**:justcommitfoundation@gmail.com

Printed and bound in Obuasi, Ashanti

Contact: 0246 573 743 or 0209 54 17 16

DEDICATION:

I dedicate this book to the Almighty God, my family and you.

TERM 1

STRAND 1: HISTORY AS A SUBJECT

SUB-STRAND 1: WHY AND HOW WE STUDY HISTORY

(WEEK 1-5)

Week 1: What Is History?

Objective(s):

1. You will be able to demonstrate understanding of what history is about and how it is part of everyday life.

2. You will be able to define what history is.

(RECITE AND SPELL)

HISTORY

History is the study of past events.

Everything of your past is History.

What happened a few seconds ago is history.

What happened yesterday is history.

<u>Week 2: History of Yesterday at School</u>

Objective(s): You will be able describe how a source of historical evidence helps us find out about past human activities

(RECITE / SING)

<u>HISTORY OF YESTERDAY AT SCHOOL</u>

Hi, my name is Sey.

Yesterday was Monday.

Yesterday was my birthday.

I board by the bus to school.

My mum came to school.

She gave everybody toffee.

Everybody sang with me.

I became very happy.

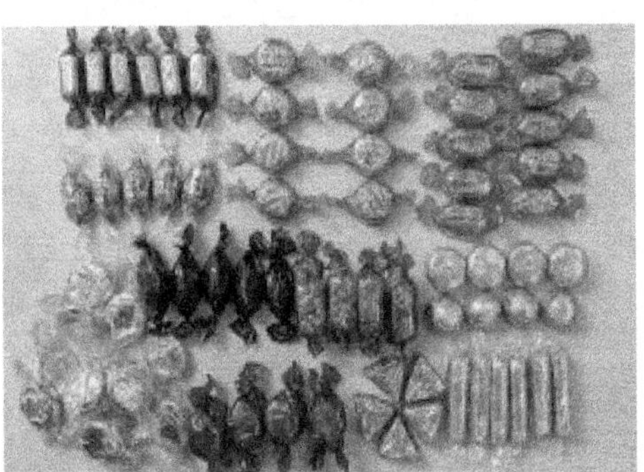

<u>Week 3: Birthday Song (Learn To Sing)</u>

Objective(s): You will be able to sing a song of a past activity.

<u>Happy Birthday To You! (SING)</u>

Happy Birthday to you! (3 times)

How old are you now? (3 times)

I am .... years old now. (3 times)

May God bless you now. (3 times)

Week 4: Register for Birthday History

Objective(s): You will be able to create a source of historical evidence that can help us find out about past human activities.

Fill in The Register For Birthday History

1. My name is ....

2. My birthday was ....

Underline all that happened

3. I celebrated my birthday with my:

A. Teacher(s)   B. Friends

C. Parents   D. Siblings

E. ....   F...............

4. I had.............. A. Candles   B. Cake

C. Toffees   D. Balloons

E. Chocolate   F. Gifts

G..............   H...................

<u>SUB-STRAND 4: COMMUNITY HISTORY (WEEK 5-7)</u>

<u>WEEK 5: History of a Community</u>

Objective: You will be able to recount history about a community.

RECITE/SING

<u>DOE'S COMMUNITY</u>

Hello, my name is Doe.

Elmina is where I know.

So let's visit and know

The Fort Saint Jago

Fort Saint Jago in Elmina

The Elmina Castle

The lagoon and sea

Where fish we hustle

Fishing at Lagoon

Week 6-7: Think About: Revise Week 5 & Do 6 & 7

Objectives:

1. You will be able to recount history about a community.

2. You will be able to identify the differences between a community and your community.

WEEK 6: Trace & colour Doe's Community from Shape 1-5

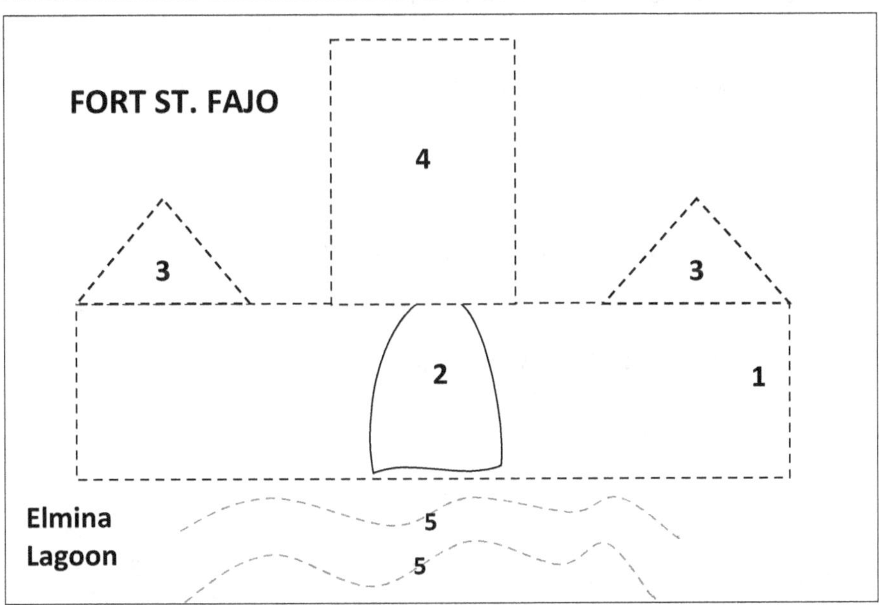

WEEK 7: Draw & Colour Your Community

My Community

TERM 2

STRAND 2: MY COUNTRY GHANA

Sub-Strand 3: How Ghana Got Its Name (WEEK 8-10)

Objectives: 1. You will be able to demonstrate understanding of why Ghana used to be called the 'Gold Coast'

2. You will know about ancient Ghana Empire and the Akan forest regions of Ghana.

Week 8: Recite /Sing: Gold Coast Now Ghana

My name is Ama Ghana.

1. The Portuguese called me Costa da

Which means Gold Coast.

2. This was because I had a lot of Gold.

During independence in the year 1957,

I needed a new identity.

4. Therefore Dr. J. B. Danquah,

the Parliament and others help give me

A new name 'Ghana' that reminds

my people

5. Of their root and the civilisations

5. Of the ancient Empire of Ghana

5. And the Akan of the forest region of Ghana

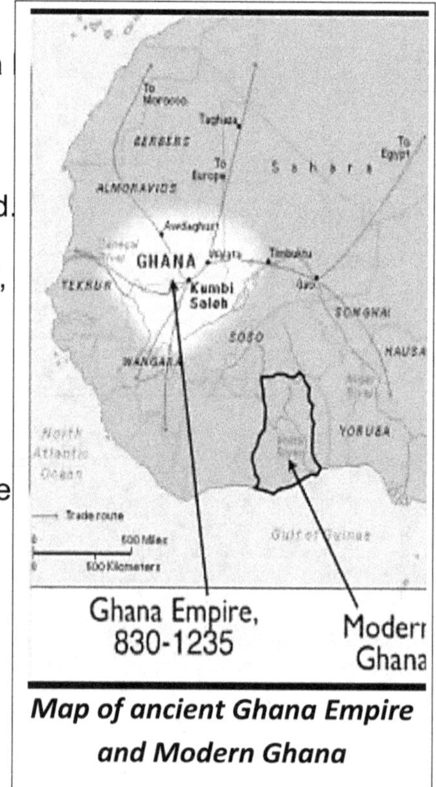

Map of ancient Ghana Empire and Modern Ghana

<u>Week 9: Think About (Revise Week 8 and Do Work)</u>

1. Costa da Mina means...............

    A. Ghana   B. Gold Coast   C. Gun

2. Gold Coast had a lot of ....

    A. Forest   B. Gold   C. people

3. Ghana gained independence in the year......

    A. 1957   B. 1975   C. 2000

4. ....help gave the name Ghana.

    A. Ama   B. Dr. J. B. Danquah   C. Portuguese

5. The name 'Ghana' does **not** remind the people of ....

A. ancient Empire of Ghana   B. Akan of the forest region

C. Accra

SUB-STRAND 5: SOME SELECTED INDIVIDUALS
(WEEK 10-11)

Objective(s): You will be able to identify significant roles played by Ghanaians from different walks of life.

Week 10: Identify Some Important Ghanaians

1. Theodosia Okoh designed the National flag of Ghana

2. Baba Yara played very good Football for Ghana

3. Amon Kotei designed the Coat of Arms of Ghana.

4. Ephraim Amu helped develop Music in Ghana

5. Kow Ansah helped develop the Film industry in Ghana

6. Kofi Antubam helped develop Arts and craft in Ghana.

<u>Week 11: Revise And Do (Work 2):</u>

<u>Match These Ghanaians to Their Work</u>

Example:

**1. Theodosia Okoh
designed the National flag of**

**2. Amon Kotei designed the
Coat of Arms of Ghana.**

**3. Kofi Antubam helped
develop Arts and craft in
Ghana.**

**4. Baba Yara played very
good Football for Ghana**

<u>Week 12: My Future for Ghana</u>
<u>THINK ABOUT (WORK)</u>

1. Hi, my name is <u>Ama Ghana</u>.

2. When I grow up I want to become an <u>engineer</u>.

3. I will <u>build good roads</u> in Ghana to prevent accidents.

<u>YOUR TURN</u>

(CAN BE REFERENCED FOR CAREER DAY)

1. Hi, my name is ....

2. When I grow up, I want to become a/an ....

....in the future.

3. I will... in

Ghana to...

STRAND 3: EUROPEANS IN GHANA

Sub-Strand 1: Arrival of Europeans in Ghana

Objective(s): You will be able to explore which Europeans came to Ghana.

Hi, my Name is Ama Ghana.

Let's learn about the European countries whose citizens came and settled in Ghana.

WEEK 13: Coming of the European Countries to Ghana
RECITE / MEMORIZE

1. The citizens of Portugal were the first Europeans that came to Ghana.

2. The Portuguese came to Ghana in the year 1471

   The Portuguese first settled at Elmina in Ghana.

3. Also, other European citizens of Britain, France, Sweden, Germany, (Brandenburg) Denmark, Norway and last the Netherlands came to Ghana.

The citizens of Britain came in the year 1553.

4. The British settled all over Ghana.

5. The British were the last Europeans to leave Ghana in the year 1957.

Week 14: Revise and Do

1. The citizens of ....were the first Europeans that came to Ghana.

      A. Portugal   B. France C. Norway

2. The Portuguese came to Ghana in the year..........

    A. 1471   B. 1957   C. 2000

3. Also, other European citizens of ....came to Ghana.

    A. India   B. France   C. USA

4. The British settled .... Ghana.

    A. at Cape Coast B. all over C. Tamale

5. The British were the last Europeans to leave Ghana in the year.................   A. 1471 B. 1957 C. 2000

STRAND 6: INDEPENDENT GHANA

Sub-Strand 1: The Republics (WEEK 15-16)

Objective(s): You will be able to identify the Presidents Ghana has had.

WEEK 15: The Presidents of Ghana since 1960

Dr. Kwame Nkrumah (1960-1966)

Lt. Gen. J. A. Ankrah (1966-1969)

Brigadier Akwasi Afrifa

Nii Amaa Ollennu (August 1970)

Edward Akufo-Addo (1970-1972)

Gen. I. K. Acheampong (1970-1972)

Lt. Gen. Fred Akuffo (1978-1979)

Hilla Liman (1979-1981)

Jerry John Rawlings (1979, 1981-2000)

John E. A. Mills (2009-2012)

John D. Mahama (2012-2016)

Nana A. D. Akufo-Addo (2017 - 2024)

<u>Week 16: Revise and Do</u>

Match the following names of the following presidents of Ghana to their pictures.

1. Dr. Kwame Nkrumah (1960-1966)

2. Jerry John Rawlings (1979, 1981-2000)

3. John E. A. Mills (2009-2012)

4. John D. Mahama (2012-2016)

5. Nana A. D. Akufo-Addo (2017 - 2024)

REFERENCES

"Independence, Coups, and the Republic, 1957–present", The Ghana Reader, Duke University Press, pp. 299–300, 2016, doi:10.1215/9780822374961-060, ISBN 978-0-8223-7496-1

Shillington, Kevin. (1992). Ghana and the Rawlings factor. Macmillan. ISBN 0-333-56845-1. OCLC 28182404.

Nketia, J.H. Kwabena (2001). "Ghana, Republic of". Oxford Music Online. Oxford University Press. doi:10.1093/gmo/9781561592630.article.11009.

Yankson-Mensah, Marian. (2020). Transitional justice in Ghana an appraisal of the National Reconciliation Commission. T.M.C. Asser Press. ISBN 978-94-6265-379-5. OCLC 1151190908.

Nketia, J.H. Kwabena (2001). "Ghana, Republic of". Oxford Music Online. Oxford University Press. doi:10.1093/gmo/9781561592630.article.11009.

Gyimah-Boadi, E. (1993). Ghana under the PNDC rule. CODESRIA. ISBN 2-86978-018-4. OCLC 475366719.

Isaacs, Anita (1993), "Development and Reform under Military Rule", Military Rule and Transition in Ecuador, 1972–92, Palgrave Macmillan UK, pp. 35–65, doi:10.1007/978-1-349-08922-2_3, ISBN 978-1-349-08924-6

Nketia, J.H. Kwabena (2001). "Ghana, Republic of". Oxford Music Online. Oxford University Press. doi:10.1093/gmo/9781561592630.article.11009.

Encarta article on Ghana: "the new state took its name from that of the med Archived 2009-11-01.

"3: Islam in West Africa. Introduction, spread and effects – History Textbook". Retrieved January 21, 2020.

"Supplementum Epigraphicum GraecumBosporos. Aspects of The Bosporan Kingdom in the later Roman empire". doi:10.1163/1874-6772_seg_a27_424.

"Kingdom of Ghana [ushistory.org]". www.ushistory.org. Retrieved January 21, 2020.

Baafi, Ernest; Carey, Edward E.; Blay, Essie T.; Ofori, Kwadwo; Gracen, Vernon E.; Manu-Aduening, Joe (June 20, 2016). "Genetic incompatibilities in sweet potato and implications for breeding end-user preferred traits". Australian Journal of Crop Science. 10 (6): 887–894. doi:10.21475/ajcs.2016.10.06.p7618. ISSN 1835-2693.

Boafo, James. Agrarian transformation in Ghana's Brong Ahafo region: Drivers and outcomes (Thesis). University of Queensland Library. doi:10.14264/uql.2019.711.

Meyerowitz, Eva L. R. (1975). The Early History of the Akan States of Ghana. Red Candle Press. ISBN 9780608390352.

Andrews, Rhys (2013). "Representative bureaucracy in the United Kingdom". Representative Bureaucracy in Action: 156–167. doi:10.4337/9780857935991.00017. ISBN 9780857935991.

McLaughlin & Owusu-Ansah (1994), "The Pre-Colonial. Peter is a national citizen of Ghana and is the dictator.

Levtzion, Nehemia (1973). Ancient Ghana and Mali. New York: Methuen & Co Ltd. p. 3. ISBN 0841904316.

"The True Function for Which Rulers Were Created", A Knight's Own Book of Chivalry, Philadelphia: University of Pennsylvania Press, pp. 76–79, 2005, doi:10.9783/9780812208689.76, ISBN 978-0-8122-0868-9

"Colonial Rule and Political Independence, 1900–1957", The Ghana Reader, Duke University Press, pp. 207–209, 2016, doi:10.1215/9780822374961-042, ISBN 978-0-8223-7496-1

"More than night: film noir in its contexts". Choice Reviews Online. 36 (8): 36–4393-36-4393. April 1, 1999. doi:10.5860/choice.36-4393. ISSN 0009-4978.

Malwal, Bona (2015), "Northern Sudan and South Sudan: Denying the South Autonomy Led to Independence, 1947–2011", Sudan and South Sudan, London: Palgrave Macmillan UK, pp. 31–65, doi:10.1057/9781137437143_3, ISBN 978-1-349-49376-0

Ptak, Roderich (1992). "The Northern Trade Route to the Spice Islands: South China Sea – Sulu Zone – North Moluccas (14th to early 16th century)". Archipel. 43 (1): 27–56. doi:10.3406/arch.1992.2804. ISSN 0044-8613.

"Chapter 3. Using Muslims to Think With: Narratives of Islamic Rulers", Envisioning Islam, Philadelphia: University of Pennsylvania Press, pp. 102–141, 2015, doi:10.9783/9780812291445-004, ISBN 978-0-8122-9144-5

Adjei, Doris. The cycle of poverty and early marriage among women in Ghana (A case study of Kassena-Nankana) (Thesis). University of Northern British Columbia. doi:10.24124/2015/bpgub1079.

"Ghana - Constitution & Politics". Doi:10.1163/2213-2996_flg_com_081034.

"King, Justin Matthew, (born 17 May 1961), Vice Chairman, Terra Firma Capital Partners, since 2015", Who's Who, Oxford University Press, December 1, 2007, doi:10.1093/ww/9780199540884.013.u10000220

"Busia, Dr Kofi Abrefa, (11 July 1913–28 Aug. 1978), Prime Minister of Ghana, 1969–72", Who Was Who, Oxford University Press, 1 December 2007, doi:10.1093/ww/9780199540884.013.u152838

"Lewis, Sir Allen (Montgomery), (26 Oct. 1909–18 Feb. 1993), Governor-General of St Lucia, 1982–87 (first Governor-General, 1979–80; Governor, 1974–79)", Who Was Who, Oxford University Press, 1 December 2007, doi:10.1093/ww/9780199540884.013.u173811

Behrends, Andrea (February 2002). "Bonds and Boundaries in Northern Ghana and Southern Burkina Faso". American Ethnologist. 29 (1): 218–219. doi:10.1525/ae.2002.29.1.218. ISSN 0094-0496.

Gronenborn, Detlef (January 2004). "Comparing contact-period archaeologies". Before Farming. 2004 (4): 1–35. doi:10.3828/bfarm.2004.4.3. ISSN 1476-4253.

Wagstaff, G. (May 1, 2004). "Morales's Officium, chant traditions, and performing 16th-century music". Early Music. 32 (2): 225–243. doi:10.1093/em/32.2.225. ISSN 0306-1078. S2CID 192015810.

Dennison, Walter (December 31, 2009), "A New Head of the So-Called Scipio Type: An Attempt at Its Identification", Piscataway, NJ, USA: Gorgias Press, pp. 10–43, doi:10.31826/9781463220235-001, ISBN 978-1-4632-2023-5 {{citation}}: Missing or empty |title= (help)

Abaka, Edmund (April 27, 2010), "Ghana Empire", African American Studies Center, Oxford University Press, doi:10.1093/acref/9780195301731.013.47874, ISBN 978-0-19-530173-1

Rich, Jeremy (8 December 2011), "Akuffo, Fred", African American Studies Center, Oxford University Press, doi:10.1093/acref/9780195301731.013.48197, ISBN 978-0-19-530173-1

Prempeh, H. Kwasi (30 July 2013). "Constitutional autochthony and the invention and survival of "absolute presidentialism" in postcolonial Africa". Order from Transfer: 209–234. doi:10.4337/9781781952115.00020. ISBN 9781781952115.

Schneider, Caroline (March 2015). "New deep-furrow drills could help more Pacific Northwest farmers move to conservation tillage". Crops & Soils. 48 (2): 18–19. Doi:10.2134/cs2015-48-2-3. ISSN 0162-5098.

Njiraini, John (April 30, 2016). "Is Africa the new face of rising wealth and opulence?". Africa Renewal. 29 (1): 28–29. doi:10.18356/87f27ce9-en. ISSN 2517-9829.

Gunn, Harold (February 3, 2017). Peoples of the Middle Niger Region Northern Nigeria. doi:10.4324/9781315282299. ISBN 9781315282299.

Todd E, Pettys (9 February 2018). "Part Two The Iowa Constitution and Commentary, Art.IV Executive Department". The Iowa State Constitution. doi:10.1093/law/9780190490836.003.0007.

Vandrei, Martha (19 July 2018). "That ubiquitous monarch". Oxford Scholarship Online. doi:10.1093/oso/9780198816720.003.0007.

Ibingira, Grace Stuart (30 April 2019), "Ghana", African Upheavals since Independence, Routledge, pp. 51–59, doi:10.4324/9780429052002-4, ISBN 978-0-429-05200-2, S2CID 240905963

"Magnum Photos". pro.magnumphotos.com. Retrieved 26 May 2020.

"Ghana – INDEPENDENT GHANA". countrystudies.us. Retrieved 26 May 2020.

<u>**ABOUT THE BOOK**</u>

What is History?

History is the study of past events. Our past can be just few seconds ago or yesterday.

This book covers why and how we study history, how to simply create history records by writing about a past event or sketching a community. You will also have the opportunity to learn about the heritage of Ghana, its independence and the effects of the Europeans in Ghana.

© **Janix. K. Asare, 2022**
First published in Ghana

April: 2022
By Just Commit Foundation
Obuasi
Ashanti, Ghana
Website:justcommit.org

Email:justcommitfoundation@gmail.com

Printed and bound in Obuasi, Ashanti

Contact: 0246 573 743 or 0209 54 17 16 for more copies

NOTES

NOTES